# THE TECHNOLOGY OF

# BASEBALL

by Thomas K. Adamson

HIGH-TECH SPORTS

CAPSTONE PRESS
a capstone imprint

Sports Illustrated Kids High-Tech Sports are published by Capstone Press,
1710 Roe Crest Drive, North Mankato, Minnesota 56003
www.capstonepub.com

**Library of Congress Cataloging-in-Publication Data**
Adamson, Thomas K., 1970–
    The technology of baseball / by Thomas K. Adamson.
        p. cm.—(Sports illustrated kids. High-tech sports)
    Includes bibliographical references and index.
    Summary: "Discusses the forms of technology that has revolutionized the game of baseball"
    —Provided by publisher.
    ISBN 978-1-4296-9955-6 (library binding)
    ISBN 978-1-62065-906-9 (paperback)
    1. Baseball—Juvenile literature.  I. Title.
    GV867.5.A336 2013
    796.357—dc23                          2012033622

**Editorial Credits**
Anthony Wacholtz, editor; Veronica Scott and Sarah Bennett, designers; Eric Gohl, media researcher;
Eric Manske production specialist

**Photo Credits**
AP Images: Al Behrman, 33, Amy Sancetta, 45, Dave Martin, 10, 11, Eric Risberg, 42, Four Seam Images/
David Welker, 44; Capstone: Eric Gohl, 27; Corbis: *San Francisco Chronicle*/Frederic Larson, 9; Courtesy
of Sportvision: 12, 13, 14, 15 (top), 16, 38; Dreamstime: Keith Clack, 35; Getty Images: Andy Hayt, 5,
Bloomberg/Jeremy Bales, 39, Michael Zagaris, 6, MLB Photos/Rich Pilling, 31, Ronald Martinez, 36;
Newscom: Icon SMI/Chris Williams, 15 (bottom), Icon SMI/Patrick S. Blood, 43, MCT, 24, MCT/John
Sleezer, 40–41; Shutterstock: Alex Staroseltsev, cover (background), 1, 21; *Sports Illustrated*: Al Tielemans, 7,
22, 28, 32, 34, Damian Strohmeyer, 8, 17, John Biever, 19, 29, 37, Robert Beck, cover, 4, 20, 23, 26, 30, Simon
Bruty, 25
Design Elements: Shutterstock

# TABLE OF CONTENTS

# HIGH-TECH BASEBALL

A manager eyes the radar gun: 92 miles per hour. The opposing pitcher's fastball is slowing down. At the start of the game, the pitcher was throwing 97-mph heaters. Now in the sixth inning, he seems to be getting tired.

The manager's team has a runner on second base with two outs in a tie game. The opposing manager leaves the pitcher in, wanting him to finish off the inning before bringing in a reliever.

The next batter due up has a batting average of .260, and only .210 against this pitcher. The manager decides to bring in a pinch hitter. He goes with an experienced contact hitter whose batting average against this pitcher is .335.

The hitter waits for his pitch. After throwing a couple curveballs, the pitcher tries a high fastball. As expected, it's slower than his best fastball and not high enough. The hitter slams it up the middle for a base hit, and the runner scores.

How did the manager know the best player to pinch hit? His tablet computer already crunched the numbers for him before the game. He used the information to make decisions throughout the game.

Faster computers allow players, managers, and fans to study more information than ever. Pro ball clubs want as many stats as they can get to help make game-time decisions. Players get in on game prep too. An exclusive **application** called Sport Pitch Review allows players to get video of any game. They can see, for example, how a relief pitcher has performed in his last 10 outings against right-handed batters. It's like getting an instant scouting report.

However, this technology has limitations. Smartphones and computer tablets are not allowed in the dugouts. But technology can help a manager be prepared to make the right move at a key point in the game.

Baseball players can watch videos of opposing pitchers and hitters to give them an edge in an upcoming game.

**application**—a computer program that performs a certain task; an application is also called an app

## CHAPTER 1

## GAME PREP

There's nothing new about pro baseball players using video. But sitting in a dark room watching a flickering film is a thing of the past. New digital video technology, smaller computers, and smartphones make this kind of prep easier and quicker to do. Coaches can even find out the best places to position fielders for each batter. Computers are better than ever at crunching data about where hitters usually hit the ball. Fielders can get into position to have a better chance to get the batter out.

Oakland Athletics players conduct last-minute research on their tablet computers before a game.

For example, David Ortiz is a left-handed pull hitter. He tends to pull the ball toward right field. Knowing that, infielders shift to their left to have a better chance of preventing Ortiz from getting a base hit on that side. The shortstop often plays on the right side of second base, and the first baseman is only a couple of feet from the foul line. Of course, Ortiz knows this strategy and sometimes tries to hit to the opposite field.

# IN THE GAME

Hitters prepare for games by hitting balls launched at them from pitching machines. Most of these machines can simulate multiple pitches. But one pitching machine goes a step further: A screen shows video of a pitcher. The batter can practice with the feel of actually being pitched to, even by the pitcher he'll face in the next game.

Technology helps players learn these general tendencies while on a plane or in a hotel room before a game. It also helps with really specific stats too. Players and coaches can find a pitcher's WHIP with runners in scoring position against right-handed batters—during night games.

## FACT

WHIP is a good measure of a pitcher's ability to get batters out.

WHIP = Walks + Hits / Innings Pitched

# MOTION CAPTURE TECHNOLOGY

Mariano Rivera has been a dominant closer for the New York Yankees for many years. The Movement Lab at New York University did a study of Rivera's pitches to figure out why no one seems to be able to hit his nasty cut fastball. The lab uses the same technology that the makers of the movie *Avatar* used.

Sensors are placed on different parts of a pitcher's arms and legs. The sensors are connected to a computer. The computer then makes a 3D model of the pitcher's movements. The player and coaches can study the player's movements to see what's working well. They can also see what he should change about his technique to make him better or avoid injury. Only the slow motion computer model can show them that detail.

Mariano Rivera

Players can record their technique when they are at their best. Then when they hit a slump, they can compare their flawed technique to their original technique and see what they are doing wrong. What player wouldn't want the chance to reduce the length of a slump?

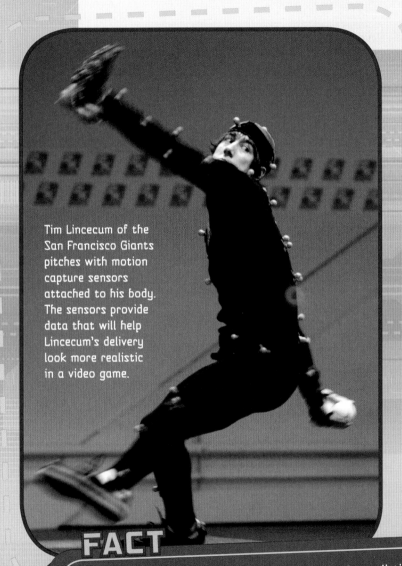

Tim Lincecum of the San Francisco Giants pitches with motion capture sensors attached to his body. The sensors provide data that will help Lincecum's delivery look more realistic in a video game.

## FACT

Motion capture technology is also used to make realistic video games. Someday a computer might be able to generate a holograph of a player's movements. This could certainly be useful in preparations for a game, but think of the possibilities for video games. Maybe you'll try to connect with a holographic Nolan Ryan pitch or try to strike out a 3D Babe Ruth!

# BIOMECHANICS

When studying a pitcher in slow motion, you might be amazed that his arm doesn't fall off when he pitches. Pitching is an aggressive motion. From the time a pitcher plants his lead foot to when he releases the ball, a mere 0.145 seconds elapses. The ball accelerates from 4 to 85 miles (6.4 to 137 kilometers) per hour or more during that short time.

The American Sports Medicine Institute

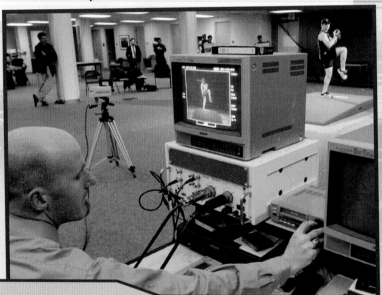

Pitching is a chain of motion: the windup, cocking the arm, accelerating the arm, and the follow-through. All of these movements can be measured if a pitcher is hooked up to a computer and monitored by high-speed cameras. The American Sports Medicine Institute has a complicated system of sensors, cameras, and computers that measure a pitcher's movement during a pitch. The computer can measure the amount of force on a pitcher's shoulder and elbow.

The results of this evaluation are used to help a pitcher improve and to help him reduce the risk of injury. If too much force is on his elbow during his delivery, he can change his technique. The computer makes a 3D model, and the data is compared to elite pitchers. The player and coach can review the tests and improve the player's mechanics. For example, they might notice the pitcher's plant foot is not at the right angle. That may be what's causing him to walk more batters, and there's a better chance he could injure his foot or leg at that angle.

Relief pitcher
Tyler Yates

## FACT

Another great technology used to measure pitching mechanics is a high-tech shirt. Sensors line the shirt at certain points along a pitcher's arms and back. The sensors record the pitcher's movement and send the data to a computer program. The program determines the acceleration of his arm and movements.

# PITCHf/x

In 2001 a technology company called Sportvision created K-Zone. This technology showed fans watching on TV the location of every pitch in relation to the strike zone. A graphic on the screen showed instantly where the ball crossed the plate. You can see where the pitches end up and how close those corner-of-the-plate strikes are to being called balls. A few years later, Sportvision developed another version of K-Zone called PITCHf/x. It was used throughout Major League Baseball (MLB) starting in 2007.

PITCHf/x tracks a strike from Philadelphia Phillies pitcher Cole Hamels.

# FACT

Sportvision created the yellow line that you see when watching football games to show how far a team has to go for a first down. They also created the bubble above race cars for NASCAR races that show the speed and position of each car.

With PITCHf/x, three cameras record the path of the pitch. The cameras are high above the field: one above home plate, one above the first base line, and one in centerfield. The cameras capture the location of the ball about 60 times on its way to the plate. The data show viewers where the pitch went, the type of pitch, and its speed. PITCHf/x technology is accurate to within 1 inch (2.5 centimeters).

Teams find this data useful in helping to improve their pitching. Every pitch is recorded precisely—where it hit the strike zone or how close it was to the strike zone. PITCHf/x can even estimate the break of the ball during the pitch. The actual break might be a little different because cameras still can't capture how much the ball spins. But it still helps identify the type of pitch thrown.

# BEYOND PITCHf/x

Even umpires use PITCHf/x to help them improve. They use a program called Zone Evaluation. The program uses PITCHf/x technology to help umpires improve their ball and strike calls. After each game the home plate ump gets a disk with an evaluation of all the game's pitches. Supervisors can review close calls with the umps to help them improve. They also look for trends. For example, an umpire might have missed seven pitches that were down and in that should have been called balls. The umpire can adjust his head angle or stance to be able to see that area better.

Building on the PITCHf/x system is HITf/x, which uses the same cameras to record what happens to the ball right after contact with the bat. Computer software records the speed of the ball off the bat, the angle it left the bat, and the direction it traveled. The hits can be compared to the type of pitch thrown for a better analysis of a batter's performance against certain pitches.

HITf/X shows the location of pitches and whether the batter recorded a hit.

COMMANDf/x tracks the location of a catcher's glove for each pitch. This software helps coaches see how much command the pitcher has of his pitches. If the catcher sets up inside but the pitch is way outside, then the pitcher's command and accuracy may be off. The analysis also helps coaches understand how well the catcher is calling the game. The location of his mitt can show where he called for a pitch.

Clayton Kershaw misses his target, brushing Ian Stewart away from the plate.

# FIELDf/x

FIELDf/x takes PITCHf/x technology and applies it to the actions of the fielders. Several 5-**megapixel** cameras capture the location of the ball and each player 15 times per second.

The cameras, accurate to within 1 foot (30 centimeters), are positioned at various places around the ballpark. Information is recorded about the players' movements, how hard the ball was hit, and the path of the ball. For each game about 2 **terabytes** of data are recorded.

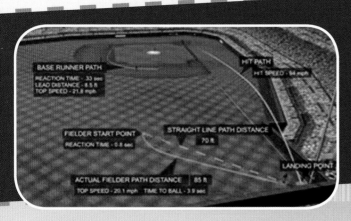

BASE RUNNER PATH
REACTION TIME - .33 sec
LEAD DISTANCE - 8.5 ft
TOP SPEED - 21.8 mph

HIT PATH
HIT SPEED - 94 mph

FIELDER START POINT
REACTION TIME - 0.8 sec

STRAIGHT LINE PATH DISTANCE
70 ft

LANDING POINT

ACTUAL FIELDER PATH DISTANCE    85 ft
TOP SPEED - 20.1 mph    TIME TO BALL - 3.9 sec

An example from the FIELDf/x program shows the paths of a fly ball and the outfielder tracking it.

## FACT

A digital file for one song is about 5 megabytes. That means it would take about 400,000 songs to add up to 2 terabytes.

**megapixel**—a measure of how much computer memory a digital picture uses; 1 megapixel equals 1 million pixels
**terabyte**—a measure of data; 1 terabyte equals 1,000 gigabytes

Teams normally adjust their defensive strategy based on instinct. For example, the Atlanta Braves' Michael Bourn is a fast base runner. Outfielders make sure to throw the ball quickly back to the infield so he doesn't try to stretch a single into a double. FIELDf/x gives teams data on how fast the runner can make it to second base. With that information, the outfielder already knows whether he has a chance to throw him out.

◄ Michael Bourn

Tagging a fielder with an error is a judgment call by the game's statistician. But FIELDf/x data can make that decision based on numbers. It tracks a player's jump on the ball and how fast the ball was traveling. Then the system compares that play to similar ones to see whether most other players could have stopped, thrown, or caught the ball successfully.

# PITCHSIGHT

PitchSight is another analysis tool that helps pitchers improve their mechanics and effectiveness. Based on missile-tracking technology, PitchSight uses two cameras that send data to a computer program. The program tracks a pitcher's release point, pitch speed, arm angle, break of the pitch, and location of the pitch.

A pitcher can do practice throws in the bullpen, then immediately see what he might be doing wrong. If his breaking pitch hasn't been working lately, the analysis can show him why. He might need to change his release so that the ball breaks differently.

## GYROBALL— A Computer-Generated Superpitch?

The gyroball was hyped as a new mysterious pitch in the mid-2000s. Kazushi Tezuka, a Japanese trainer, was said to have invented the gyroball. He worked with Ryutaro Himeno, a computer scientist, who simulated the pitch using computer models.

The idea behind a gyroball makes it a unique pitch. Unlike a fastball or a curveball, it spins sideways. In practice, it's between a fastball and a breaking ball. Because of the ball's sideways spin, it doesn't break as a slider would. It cruises straight at the batter, who might be thinking fastball, but then the ball drops a bit quicker than a fastball. But it doesn't drop as much as a curveball.

Some major league pitchers claim to be able to throw a gyroball. Others say it's impossible. Some pitchers say it's possible but extremely difficult to control. The gyroball remains a pitch surrounded in mystery!

Without the analysis, pitchers would continue to do the same thing and possibly get hammered by batters. The other option would be to experiment with different styles until something worked. PitchSight allows pitchers to make adjustments before the next game, providing quicker results.

Pitchers work on their mechanics during bullpen sessions between games.

# HOW TO HIT A HOME RUN

Every hitter likes fastballs. If they're in the strike zone, most good hitters can get a bat on them. But you don't earn a career batting average over .300 by hitting only fastballs. A player has to contend with everything pitchers throw at him.

According to one study, if you want to hit the ball farther, you might prefer curveballs. The study showed that a perfectly hit curveball will go farther than a perfectly hit fastball. The scientists doing the study used many calculations and considered numerous factors. They looked at the bat and ball's mass, the speed of the pitch, the speed of the bat, the angle of the swing, the ball's spin, and gravity.

The study started with the idea that a ball hit up in the air likely has backspin. A ball with backspin has more **lift**. The effect is minor, but the ball will travel farther if it has backspin. A fastball spins backward as it speeds toward the batter. So when the batter hits a fastball into the air, the ball's rotation is reversed. That slight loss of energy in changing the ball's spin means the ball doesn't go quite as far.

A curveball, however, comes at the batter with topspin. When it's hit in the air, the ball has backspin, so it's spinning with maximum lift after the hit. Undercutting the ball adds to that spin, which increases the lift as the ball heads over the outfield fence.

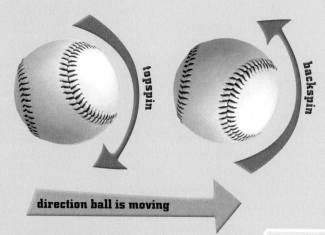

topspin

backspin

direction ball is moving

lift—the upward force that causes an object to rise in the air

# BAT SPEED

Coaches tell players to increase their bat speed to become better hitters. Technology proves this is good advice. A study found that increasing bat speed helps a batter hit the ball farther than if he used a heavier bat. Against a 94-mph (151-km) fastball, every 1-mile- (1.6-km-) per-hour increase in bat speed sends the ball 8 feet (2.4 m) farther. That could be the difference between an out and a home run.

Bats can weigh the same but have different swing weights. A bat's swing weight is how heavy the bat feels when you swing it. In science that's called the bat's moment of inertia (MOI). A bat's swing weight depends on the bat's weight and its center of gravity, called its balance point.

**moment of inertia**

Scientists use a device to measure a bat's MOI. The machine grips the bat at the handle and holds it upside down. The bat is allowed to swing back and forth like a **pendulum**. A timing system connected to the machine uses **infrared** light to measure the time it takes for one complete pendulum swing.

**pendulum**—a weight that swings back and forth
**infrared**—a type of light that is invisible to human eyes

Knowing the MOI of a few bats allowed the scientists to measure the swing speeds of players. The study showed that increasing bat speed always makes a ball go farther. But using a bat with a lower MOI doesn't have as much effect. You might get more hits because you can control the bat better, but you won't hit more home runs. A low-MOI bat has a less effective collision with the ball than a high-MOI bat. If you want to hit the ball farther, use a bat with a higher MOI (more weight in the barrel). You should also work on upper body strength, which will help you swing the bat faster.

## FACT

With aluminum bats, which are used by high school and college players, the way a bat's weight is distributed can vary greatly. The bat might have more weight toward the handle, which makes the bat feel lighter and easier to swing. Or the bat might have more weight in the barrel at the end of the bat. That makes the bat feel heavier when it's swung and gives it a higher MOI.

# TOMMY JOHN SURGERY

Pitchers rely on their ulnar collateral ligament (UCL). This ligament connects the upper arm bone to the inside lower arm bone. Pitching puts a great deal of stress on this ligament, especially when throwing breaking pitches.

In 1974 left-handed pitcher Tommy John of the Los Angeles Dodgers tore his UCL. At that time injuring the UCL meant the end of a pitcher's career. But that year Dr. Frank Jobe performed a new kind of surgery on John's elbow. The doctor replaced the torn ligament with a tendon from John's right wrist.

## Tommy John elbow surgery

*Named for the first pitcher to undergo the elbow procedure, the surgery has become relatively routine for professional baseball players.*

### What goes wrong

UCL stretches or breaks, making it impossible to gain enough speed on throw

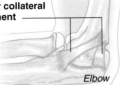

Ulnar collateral ligament — Elbow

### How to fix it

**❶** Palmaris longus tendon, a nonessential tendon about 4-6 in. (10-15 cm) long, is removed from opposite forearm

**❷** 3 mm holes are drilled into ends of the humerus and ulna bones

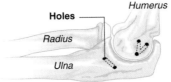

Holes — Radius — Ulna — Humerus

**❸** Tendon is woven back and forth between the holes and stitched together

Grafted palmaris longus tendon

© 2010 MCT  Source: Chicago Tribune research    Graphic: Chicago Tribune

Jobe sliced through the muscle on the inside of John's left elbow to expose the damaged ligament. Next he drilled holes in the ulna and humerus bones. He threaded the replacement tendon through the holes in a figure-8 pattern. The surgery was successful, and John pitched 14 more years and won another 164 games.

Doctors usually use a tendon from the pitcher's nonthrowing wrist to replace the UCL. Sometimes the doctor uses a tendon from the pitcher's toe or leg. A tendon from a *cadaver* can be used too.

**cadaver**—a dead body that is used for medical or scientific purposes

The surgery became known as Tommy John surgery, named for the pitcher who had so much success afterward. It takes about one year for a pitcher who has the surgery to return to competition. He has to regain his arm strength. The tendon, which is now acting as a ligament, takes time to heal into that position. It can take two years to return to his previous pitching speeds and abilities. Even then he may not be able to perform at 100 percent the rest of his career. The surgery is becoming more common, and stars such as John Smoltz, Tim Hudson, and Stephen Strasburg have made full recoveries and pitched well after having Tommy John surgeries.

Washington Nationals pitcher Stephen Strasburg bounced back strong after having Tommy John surgery in 2011. He went 15-6 in 2012 with a 3.16 ERA and 197 strikeouts in only 159.1 innings. The team wanted to be careful with their young ace, so Strasburg stopped pitching toward the end of the season.

# EQUIPMENT

## CHAPTER 2

## THE SWEET SPOT

Tapping a baseball bat with a hammer might seem like a strange way to test its performance. But the test reveals how a bat vibrates when it hits a ball. The tests help bat manufacturers make better bats that follow college and pro rules. They also help measure a bat's sweet spot.

If a bat vibrates too much when it hits a ball, the energy in the hit goes into the vibrations instead of putting force behind the ball. So fewer vibrations in the bat result in more speed and distance in the ball. These tests measure the vibrations to find out exactly where on the bat the vibrations are strongest and where they are weakest. The spot where there are no vibrations is the bat's sweet spot. Making metal bats with finely tuned sweet spots will help young players develop into better hitters. Pros, on the other hand, have to learn to see the pitches better and work on technique.

◄ Albert Pujols

Bat vibrations can also be measured with an **accelerometer**. This electronic device is attached to a bat to measure the pressure and stress on the bat caused by hitting the ball. Scientists can then see how different parts of the bat vibrate.

If you don't have an accelerometer or a computer system and hammer to measure a bat's vibration, you can still experience it firsthand. You can listen to the bat. Hold the bat lightly about 6 inches (15 cm) from the knob on the handle. Let it hang there, and put your ear close to the knob. Now tap the barrel of the bat with your finger, and listen for a hum. If you have trouble hearing it, try tapping the barrel with a baseball. Once you hear the hum, try tapping different spots. See if you can find a spot where there is no hum. That's the sweet spot.

**accelerometer**—an electronic device that measures pressure and stress

# ASH OR MAPLE BATS?

One of the reasons college and amateur baseball teams use metal bats is because they don't break. Major league clubs can afford to replace bats, so they use wood bats even though they tend to break often.

Traditionally, pro baseball players used bats made from the wood of ash trees. The wood from these trees was lighter and allowed players to swing faster.

The Louisville Slugger factory in Louisville, Kentucky

Many players today use maple bats. The wood is drier and harder, and the surface stays hard for a long period of time. The surface of an ash bat tends to flake with use.

The problem with maple bats is that they break more easily. Lumber cut with the **grain** perfectly will make tougher bats. The tree rings in ash trees make distinct lines, and the wood between the rings is denser than maple. Maple has wider rings, and the grain lines aren't as straight, which means it's more likely to splinter when it breaks.

Researchers used a machine created just for hurling baseballs at bats to find out which type of wood performed better. The Baum Hitting Machine can launch a baseball at 100 miles (161 km) per hour and swing a bat at 100 miles per hour. It generates data on a computer about the collision and calculates the exact batted ball speed. Using the machine, researchers determined that ash and maple bats perform almost the same.

# FACT

Maple bats became more widely used after 2001. That year Barry Bonds broke the single season home run record using a maple bat.

**grain**—the layers of fibers in a piece of wood

# BASEBALLS

On June 6, 1999, the Colorado Rockies were trailing the Milwaukee Brewers going into the bottom of the seventh inning. Four Rockies batters hit home runs off two Brewers pitchers in that inning. That still stands as a Rockies team record for most home runs in one inning. The Rockies went on to win the game 10-5.

Coors Field in Denver, Colorado

The Rockies' stadium had already developed a reputation for being an easy place to hit homers. Their home field is high in the mountain air of Denver, Colorado. Players enjoy hitting in the thin air, but it's a nightmare for pitchers. So in 2002 the Rockies started storing game balls in a humidor. A humidor is like a big walk-in refrigerator, except it keeps things inside warm and humid instead of cold. Humid air makes baseballs less bouncy so they don't carry as far. The humidor has reduced the number of home runs hit at the Rockies' park.

When no one is looking, could the Rockies sneak in balls that were not stored in the humidor when they're batting? Not likely. The umpires watch the bag of game balls closely. They only use approved baseballs during a game.

FACT

The Arizona Diamondbacks considered using a humidor for their home games in the very dry desert. But they found out from a mathematical study that home runs would be reduced much more than they were in Denver. So they decided not to use a humidor.

# SAFETY EQUIPMENT

Safety comes first in baseball, and safety equipment continues to improve. Players wear elbow pads, ankle guards, and batting helmets made of high-tech material. The protection is important for players' safety, but they are also designed to allow natural movement.

Most major league catchers wear regular helmets backward with catchers' masks over them. Buster Posey (right) of the San Francisco Giants wears a catcher's helmet that looks more like a hockey goalie's mask. It offers the best protection from speeding fastballs and foul tips.

A new batting helmet is required to be used in MLB in 2013. The helmet protects the batter from pitches up to 100 miles (161 km) per hour. To test the new helmet, researchers fired baseballs at it from an air cannon. The outside of the helmet is made of tough carbon fiber, a super-strong, lightweight material. Carbon fiber is strands of carbon that are thinner than human hair. The strands can be twisted together and woven into any shape. The inside of the helmet has a lot more extra padding to absorb the impact of a fastball. The interior material even absorbs moisture so the batter can keep cool.

There is one big problem with this new helmet. It's much bigger than the standard helmet, and some players think it's distracting. Even if the new helmets don't catch on, they may be a stepping stone to future helmets.

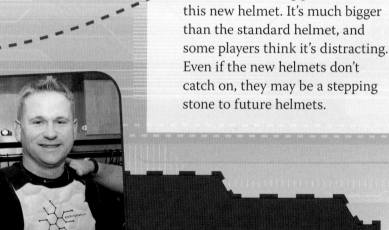

MLB umpire Mike Muchlinski is fitted with a new, cooler vest.

# UMPIRE SAFETY

Umpires need equipment to keep them safe too. Besides being hit by the occasional foul ball, umpires have to stand in the hot sun for three hours or more. Umpires wear padded vests for protection against stray balls, but what about the heat? New vests were designed with cold packs to keep umpires about 20 degrees cooler than when wearing regular vests.

# FIELD MAINTENANCE

The regular season starts at the beginning of April. Field maintenance crews in cold climates have to convince the grass that it's summer when winter is barely over.

A series of tubes lies about 1 foot (30 cm) beneath the grass at some fields. The tubes are filled with water and **glycol** to make steam, which helps control the temperature of the ground. The crew can turn up the heat in early spring to get the turf ready for opening day.

Target Field

At newer baseball parks, engineers have found ways to conserve the large amounts of water needed to maintain the lush green fields. Rainwater that falls on Target Field in Minnesota flows through an underground drainage system to a well beyond the left centerfield wall. The water is filtered and disinfected with ultraviolet light and chlorine. It can then be pumped out to water the field or to wash the seating areas.

**glycol**—a thick liquid used to keep other liquids from freezing

# FACT

In 2011 the Minnesota Twins reused 686,360 gallons (2.6 million liters) of rainwater at Target Field.

To keep a field in top condition, it needs the right amount of water. The field maintenance crew uses a soil probe to measure the depth of soil moisture. The probe helps the crew see how quickly the water reaches the roots of the grass.

Some high-tech ballparks also have sensors buried under the turf to measure moisture so that the fields get the amount of water they need. Most parks also have a sprinkler system that can pop up and water the field.

## CHAPTER 3

## BIG SCREENS AND SMALL SCREENS

It's great to be at the ballpark and see the big game in person. But if you're sitting in the top row, it might be hard to tell what's going on. That's why the big screens allow every fan to see the details of the game.

A camera records Texas Rangers pitcher Yu Darvish during a baseball game. The network places graphics, such as Darvish's stats, over the video feed.

The video boards at ballparks are getting bigger and better every year. Millions of LEDs illuminate the screens. They show enough stats, scores, and highlights for fans to keep busy between innings and during pitching changes. Some teams are starting to install high-definition screens in the ballparks, offering the best screen resolution possible.

The Kansas City Royals unveiled a new video board at Kauffman Stadium in 2008. The screen is 104 feet (32 m) tall and 84 feet (26 m) wide. It covers an area larger than the infield. It cost $8.3 million to make, and 17 people are needed to operate it.

When you're not at the stadium, you can follow the game online with MLB's Gameday. Follow every pitch and read play-by-play summaries so you don't miss any of the game. Gameday is loaded with stats. The box score is updated as the action happens so you can see how the home run Josh Hamilton just hit increased his slugging percentage. Gameday also uses PITCHf/x data to display in real time the pitch type, speed, and location in the strike zone. The strike zone display even shows a batter's hot and cold zones—where he likes to see pitches within the strike zone and where he struggles to get hits. The play-by-play summaries are archived so you can review any game you might have missed.

## FACT

An app called Ballpark Envi brings fans to any MLB stadium. The app even lets fans virtually visit stadiums that don't exist anymore, such as the historic Shibe Park in Philadelphia.

# SMARTPHONES

Countless phone apps now help diehard fans follow their favorite teams. Some apps focus on baseball news. Baseball fans only have to look in one place for the latest trades, injuries, and other news on their favorite teams. There are also apps that provide up-to-the-second stats for the fans who love numbers.

MLB At Bat provides news, stats, and broadcasts of all baseball games. It can also be customized to track only favorite teams. MLB provides a new version each season.

MLB At Bat

Topps Pennant lets fans relive classic matchups or check on games they missed. It provides the stats and play-by-play summary in an easy-to-use display. Win an argument about a key historical baseball moment. Look for classic games, such as when Roger Maris broke the single season home run record in 1961 or when Sandy Koufax pitched a perfect game in 1965. The historical games go back to 1952.

An employee of Major League Baseball Advanced Media (BAM) views video feed of several games. BAM provides streaming of pro baseball games through programs such as MLB At Bat and MLB.TV.

## AUTOMATIC TRASH TALK

One app will even create trash talk for you. Enter your favorite team and the next team they are playing, and based on current stats, the app will tell you how your team is better. Here are two examples of what the program came up with for the rivalry between Red Sox and Yankees fans:

*"The Red Sox have had more Cy Young winners over the past 20 years than the Yankees."*

*"Winning isn't everything. Oh no, wait. Yes it is, and the Yankees have a better overall record than the Red Sox this season."*

# MAKING THE RIGHT CALL

On June 1, 2011, the Kansas City Royals and the Los Angeles Angels battled for 8½ innings with no score. In the bottom of the ninth inning, Jeff Francoeur of the Royals singled with one out. Billy Butler was next to bat. He belted Scott Downs' pitch to deep left field. The ball hit a fence over the left field wall in Kauffman Stadium and bounced back into the outfield. The umpires ruled it a ground-rule double and Francoeur had to hold up at third base.

Royals manager Ned Yost immediately went onto the field to argue that it was really a home run. The umpires reviewed the instant replay of the hit. The replay video proved that the ball had cleared the fence and should have been ruled a home run. The umpires reversed their decision, and the game ended with the Royals winning 2-0.

The cameras used to track players' movements for scorekeeping and stat-keeping, as well as for watching the game on a handheld device, was put to another use: replay. MLB started using replay in 2008 to let umps check questionable home runs, such as the one that turned Billy Butler's double into a game-winning home run.

Billy Butler (16) celebrates with his teammates after the umpires reversed their call.

Baseball is a traditional sport. Some fans and players wonder if instant replay represents too much technology in the game. Expanded replay would begin to eliminate what some call the human element of the game. Umps make mistakes, and some people argue that it's part of the game. Others argue that replay and other technology would make the games even more accurate. What's ahead for officiating in baseball? Should machines call the balls and strikes? Or should real umpires continue to call the games?

Even for the biggest die-hard fans, baseball can be a slow game. There's down time between every half inning, when a new pitcher comes into the game, and during meetings at the mound. No wonder there's a seventh-inning stretch! But fans have plenty to do during the game, whether they're at home or at the park.

A phone app from MLB.com lets you check live scores and stats of your favorite baseball teams.

## FACT

No more waiting in line at the concession stand! With an app called Bypass Lane, a fan can save a trip and not miss a second of the game. The fan can place an order with a smartphone, and the food will be delivered right to his or her seat.

Fantasy baseball is a fun option for hard-core fans and casual fans alike. There are several online programs that organize stats and analyze data for you. You can take your information with you on a smartphone or tablet and make trades on the go. You can check stats as they happen with apps specially made for fantasy league players.

A fan uses his iPad to record an exciting play during the 2011 National League playoffs.

For fans who don't want to commit to an entire fantasy league, GameSlam is another option. The online game is played during the actual game. Once a game starts, fans go online and bet on various outcomes. They can bet whether a pitch will be a strike or ball, or whether the batter will get a hit or strike out. Players don't place bets with real money. They start with a certain number of points and bet an amount of points. The payout is bigger if you predict something less likely, like a triple play. Fans can play the game as often as they like. They can also leave the game before the real contest is over.

# HIGH-TECH AT ALL LEVELS

Apps and computer programs are not just for the big leagues. Phone apps can help you keep score and track stats for Little League and rec ball too. Tracking stats and generating plays has never been easier at any level.

A minor league player uses his phone to record the action of the Midwest League All-Star Home Run Derby in 2011.

Technology helps amateur, college, and even Little League teams track stats and data. It used to be time-consuming to crunch numbers after a game. Now smartphone apps allow teams to keep score electronically, which means you don't have to memorize a bunch of abbreviations or have good handwriting.

These programs also keep track of stats and organize the data for you. Need a hitter's spray chart that shows what part of the field he or she hits to most? These inexpensive programs can create that for you. You don't even need to be an expert at making hitting charts. It's much quicker now to see whether the infield should shift for a batter.

Technology helps us enjoy baseball even more. Amateurs, college players, and kids just learning the game can use inexpensive phone apps that help them study video of their pitches, swings, and even slides. With the SwingReader baseball app, you can make a video of a player and watch it in slow motion to analyze the movements. Technology has even helped ballparks conserve energy. Only time will tell how technology will continue to shape our national pastime!

In 2012 a wind turbine was constructed at Progressive Field in Cleveland, Ohio, to generate power.

## FAKE LEATHER GLOVES

People will keep using technology to try to improve the game. Although gloves have been made of leather since they first were used in the late 1800s, inventor Scott Carpenter had a different idea. He created a glove made of a synthetic microfiber that looks and feels like leather. His glove is much lighter, and he can customize each glove to fit a player's hand perfectly. The gloves are stronger than leather too.

# GLOSSARY

**accelerometer** (ak-sel-ur-OM-uh-tur)—an electronic device that measures pressure and stress

**application** (ap-li-KAY-shuhn)—a computer program that performs a certain task; an application is also called an app

**cadaver** (kuh-DAV-ur)—a dead body that is used for medical or scientific purposes

**glycol** (GLY-kol)—a thick liquid used to keep other liquids from freezing

**grain** (GRAYN)—the layers of fibers in a piece of wood

**humerus** (HYOO-mur-us)—the upper arm bone; it extends between the shoulder and elbow

**infrared** (in-frah-RED)—a type of light that is invisible to human eyes

**lift** (LIFT)—the upward force that causes an object to rise in the air

**megapixel** (MEG-uh-pik-suhl)—a measure of how much computer memory a digital picture uses; one megapixel equals 1 million pixels

**pendulum** (PEN-dyuh-luhm)—a weight that swings back and forth

**statistician** (stat-iss-TI-shun)—a person who studies numerical data

**terabyte** (TER-uh-bite)—a measure of data; 1 terabyte equals 1,000 gigabytes

**ulna** (ULL-nuh)—the lower arm bone on the little finger side of the forearm

# READ MORE

**Adamson, Thomas K.** *Baseball: The Math of the Game.* Mankato, Minn.: Capstone Press, 2012.

**Dreier, David.** *Baseball: How It Works.* Mankato, Minn.: Capstone Press, 2010.

**Fridell, Ron.** *Sports Technology.* Minneapolis: Lerner Publications, 2009.

**Hile, Lori.** *Getting Ahead: Drugs, Technology, and Competitive Advantage.* Chicago: Heinemann Library, 2012.

# INTERNET SITES

FactHound offers a safe, fun way to find Internet sites related to this book. All of the sites on FactHound have been researched by our staff.

Here's all you do:

Visit *www.facthound.com*

Type in this code: 9781429699556

 Super-cool stuff! Check out projects, games and lots more at **www.capstonekids.com**

# INDEX